Mel Bay Presents

Laurindo Almeida
Praise Every Morning

Music for Guitar & Voice

CD CONTENTS

1. Morning Has Broken [3:06]
2. Ave Maria [4:22]
3. Sweet Little Jesus Boy [3:49]
4. His Eye Is on the Sparrow [2:19]
5. A Prayer [2:50]
6. Amazing Grace [2:53]
7. Jesu, Joy of Man's Desiring [3:11]
8. Were You There When They Crucified My Lord? [4:49]
9. Jesus, Jesus Rest Your Head [3:32]
10. Nobody Knows the Trouble I've Seen [3:22]
11. What God Hath Promised [2:42]

MEL BAY

© 1996 BY MEL BAY PUBLICATIONS, INC., PACIFIC, MO 63069.
ALL RIGHTS RESERVED. INTERNATIONAL COPYRIGHT SECURED. B.M.I. MADE AND PRINTED IN U.S.A.

Visit us on the Web at http://www.melbay.com — E-mail us at email@melbay.com

Contents

Morning Has Broken 3

Ave Maria 6

Sweet Little Jesus Boy 9

His Eye Is On The Sparrow 12

A Prayer 16
    (En Prière)

Amazing Grace 20

Jesu, Joy Of Man's Desiring 24
    (from Cantata No. 147)

Were You There When They Crucified My Lord? 28
    (A Traditional Negro Spiritual)

Jesus, Jesus, Rest Your Head 30
    (A Christmas Song from the Appalachian Mountains)

Nobody Knows The Trouble I've Seen 33
    (A Traditional Negro Spiritual)

What God Hath Promised 36

Morning Has Broken

Arranged for Voice and Guitar by
   Laurindo Almeida

Lyrics: Morn-ing has bro-ken like the first morn-ing, black-bird has spo-ken like the first bird. praise for the sing-ing! praise for the morn-ing! Praise for them,

Copyright © 1996 Brazilliance Music. All Rights Reserved. Used by Permission. Exclusive Selling Agent: Mel Bay Publications, Inc.

spring - ing fresh from the Word! Sweet the rain's
¢II
new fall sun- lit from heav - en, like the first dew - fall on the first
C II
grass. praise for the sweet - ness of the wet gar - den, sprung in com-
MCV
pletes - ness where His feet pass.
rit.
Solo
C V
MC III
a'piacere
Mine is the sun - light! mine is the
H.19

morn - ing born of the one light E - den saw
C II
C IV
C II
play! Praise with e - la - tion, praise ev - 'ry
C IV
rit. 2nd time
morn - ing, God's re - cre - a - tion of a new
C IV
1.
2.
(ritard 2nd time)
day! Praise with e - day!
Hum hum hum
rit.
C II
H12 ten.
H12 ten.
H5 ten.
H5

Ave Maria

Arranged for Voice and Guitar by
Laurindo Almeida

Franz Schubert

Lento

(let bass notes ring)

A - ve Ma - ri - a! Gra - ti - a ple - na, Ma - ri - a gra - ti - a ple -
A - ve Ma - ri - a! Ma - ter de - i! O ra pro no - bis pec - ca - to - ri - bus O ra O ra pro no -
A - ve Ma - ri - a! Jung - frau mild, er - hö - re ei - ner Jung - frau Fle - hen, aus die - sem Fel - sen starr und
A - ve Ma - ri - a! Rei - ne Magd! Der Er - de und der Luft Dä - mo - nen, von dei - nes Au - ges Huld ver

Copyright © 1996 Brazilliance Music. All Rights Reserved. Used by Permission. Exclusive Selling Agent: Mel Bay Publications, Inc.

na. A - ve! A - ve Do - mi - nus, do - mi - nus te cum be - ne
bis O - ra O - ra pro no - bis, pec - ca - to - ri - bus nunc
wild, soll meih Ge - bet zu dir hin we - hen, Wir
jagt; sei kön - nen hier nicht bei - uns woh - nen! Wir

dic - ta tu in mu li e - ri - bus et be - ne - dic - tus et
et in ho - ra mor - tis in ho - ra mor - tis no - strae in
schla - fen si - cher bis zum Mor - gen, ob Men - schen noch so grau - sam sind. O
woll'n uns still dem Schick - sal beu - gen, da uns dein heil' - ger Trost an - weht; der

be - ne - dic - tus fruc - tus ven - tris ven - tris tu - i Je - su.
ho - ra mor - tis, mor - tis nos - trae in ho - ra mor - tis no - strae.
Jung - frau, sieh' der Jung - frau Sor - gen, O Mut - ter, hör ein bit - tend Kind!
Jung - frau wol - le hold dich nei - gen, dem Kind, das für den Va - ter fleht!

to Coda
A - ve Ma-ri - a!
A - ve Ma-ri - a!
A - ve Ma-ri - a!
A - ve Ma-ri - a!
MC II
D.S. al Coda
Coda
a!
a!
a!
a!
MC I
p
pp
C II
ppp

Sweet Little Jesus Boy

Arranged for Voice and Guitar by
Laurindo Almeida

Words and Music by
ROBERT MacGIMSEY

Slowly with simplicity and sincerity

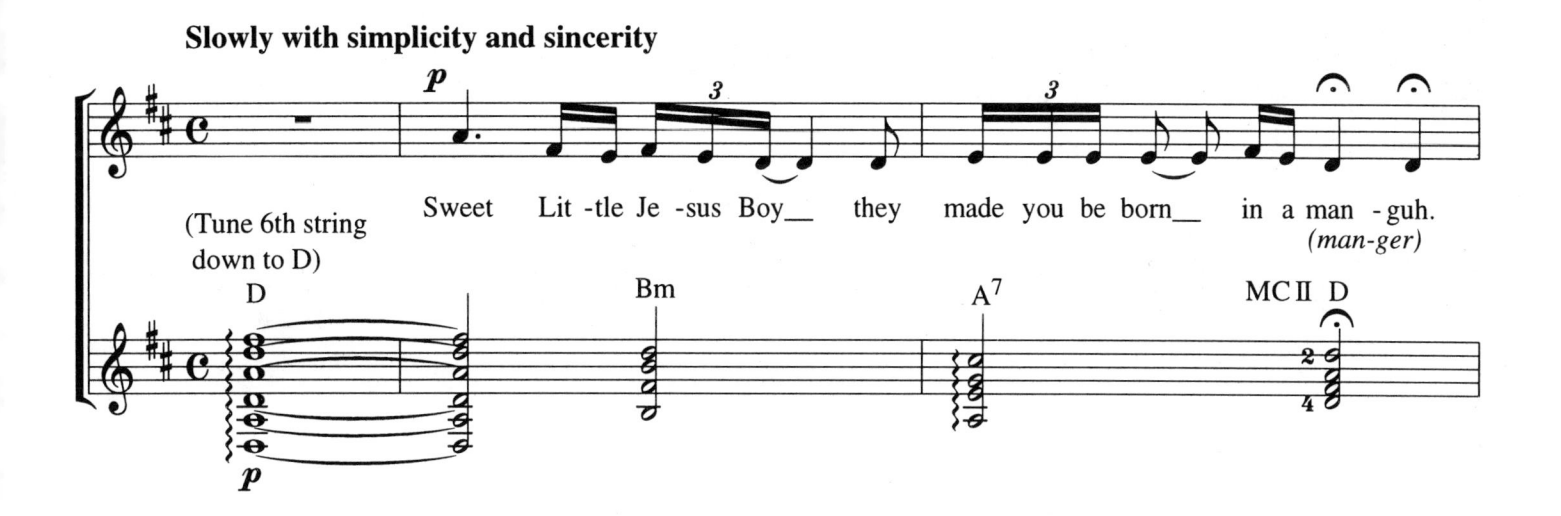

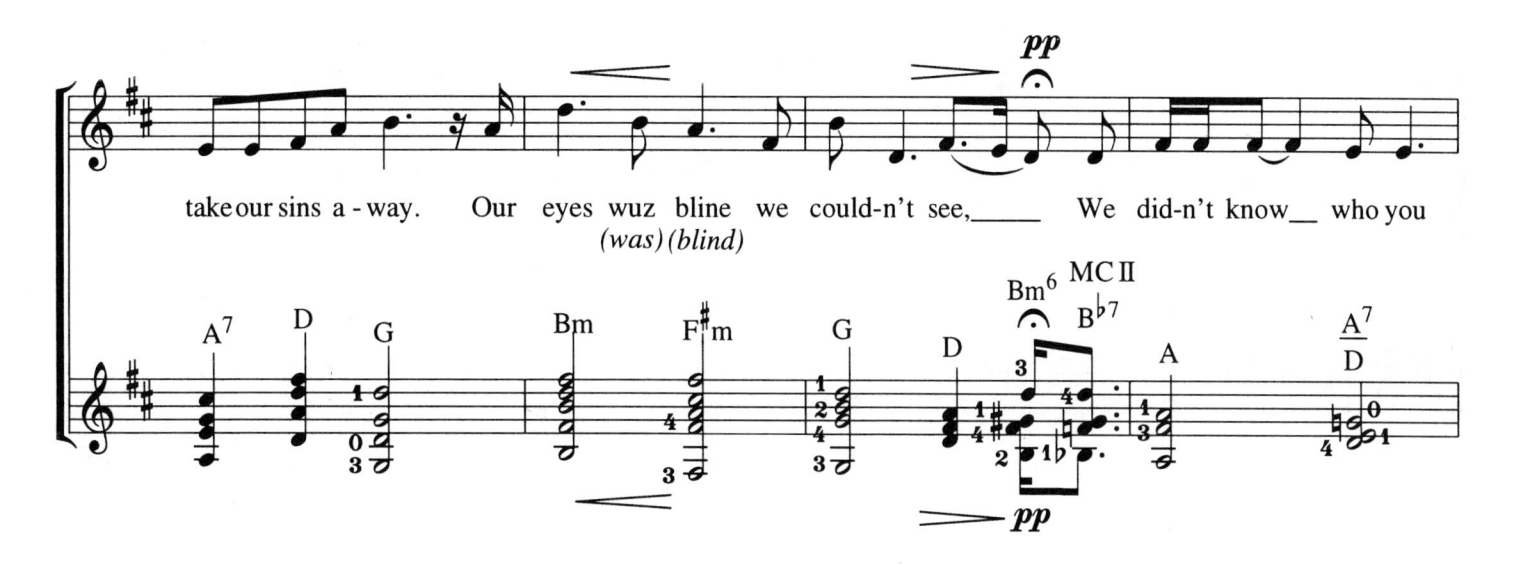

(Tune 6th string down to D)

Sweet Little Jesus Boy__ they made you be born__ in a man - guh.
(man-ger)

Sweet Little Holy Chil'__ did-n't know who you wuz. Did-n't know__ you'd come to save us Lawd; To
(was) *(Lord)*

take our sins a - way. Our eyes wuz bline we could-n't see,____ We did-n't know__ who you
(was)(blind)

Copyright © 1996 Brazilliance Music. All Rights Reserved. Used by Permission. Exclusive Selling Agent: Mel Bay Publications, Inc.

wuz. Long time a-go____ you wuz bawn,____ Bawn in a man-guh low____
(was) *(was)* *(Born)* *(man-ger)*

with sympathetic fervour

Sweet Lit-tle Je-sus Boy. De worl' treat you mean__ Lawd, treat me mean__ too, but
(The) *(world)*

tat's how__ things is down heah:__ We don't know who you is. You done__ tol' us how__
(that's) *(here)* *(told)*

we is a try-in'___ mas-tuh you__ done__ show'd us how__ eb-m when you's dy-in'.
(mas-ter) *(ev-en)* *(you was)*

(silence)

very slow
(pleadingly)
Jes seem like we kan do right, look how we treat- ed you. But please__ suh fuh- give us Lawd___ we
(just) (can't) (sir) (forgive)
A Bm F♯m A7 D G Bm F♯m/A G7 D Bm6 B♭7
Coda
pp
(under one's breath, as though talking to one's self)
did - n't know 'twas you. Sweet Lit - tle Je - sus Boy___ bawn long time a- go___
(it was) (born)
D/A A7 D D G6 D
pp
(dying away)
ppp
Sweet Lit - tle Ho - ly Chil'___ an' we did - n't know who you wuz.
(was.)
D Bm E7 D/A A7 (D) D
ppp

His Eye Is On The Sparrow

Arranged for Voice and Guitar by
Laurindo Almeida

Music by
CHARLES H. GABRIEL

I sing be-cause I'm hap-py___ I sing be-cause I'm free.___ For His eye is on the spar-row___ and I know He watch-es me.___

Why should I feel dis-cour-aged?___ Why should the

Copyright © 1996 Brazilliance Music. All Rights Reserved. Used by Permission. Exclusive Selling Agent: Mel Bay Publications, Inc.

sha - dows come? Why should my heart be
C I
lone - ly and long for heav'n and home?
When Je - sus is my por - tion My
C IV
C I
con - stant friend is He His eye is
C I
C II
C IV

on__ the spar-row_____ and I know He watch - es

me._____ His eye is on the spar - row____

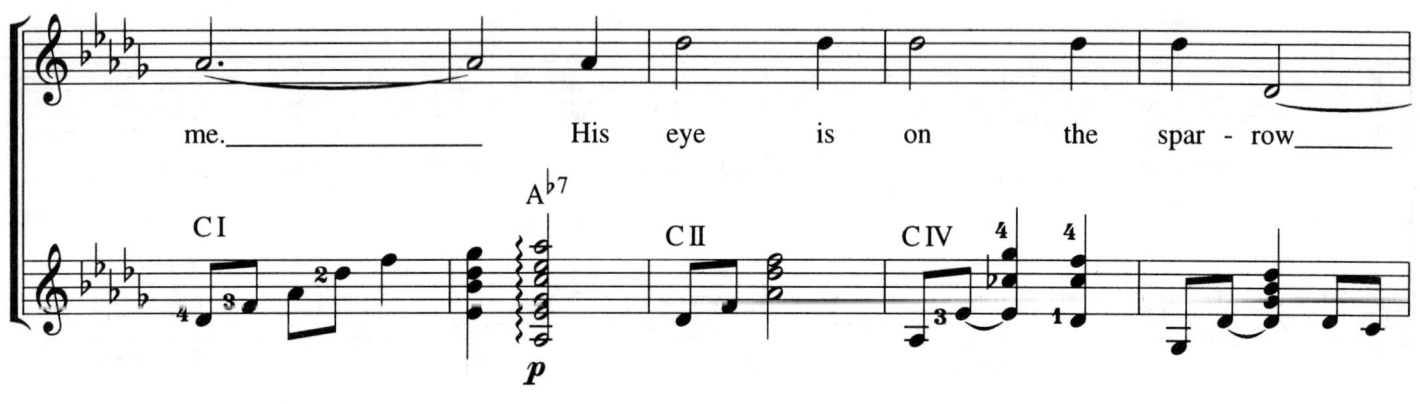

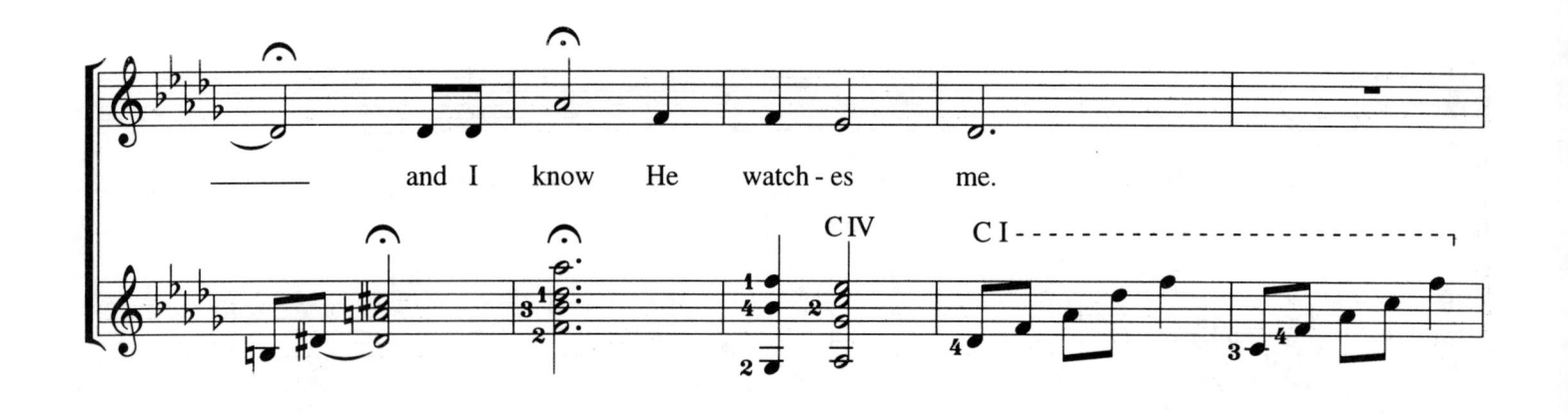

and I know He watch - es me.

Refrain

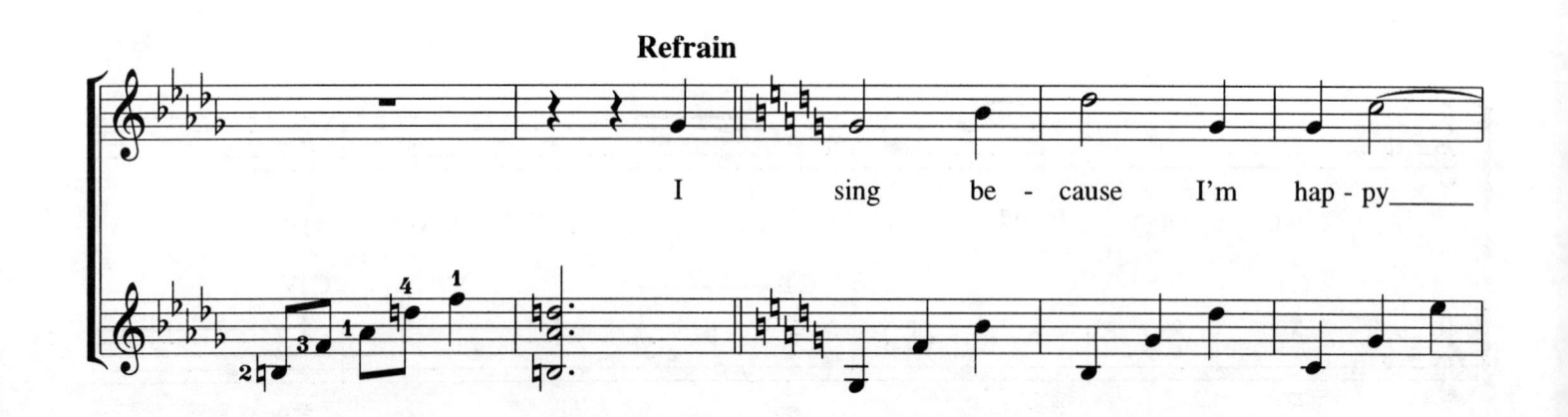

I sing be - cause I'm hap - py____

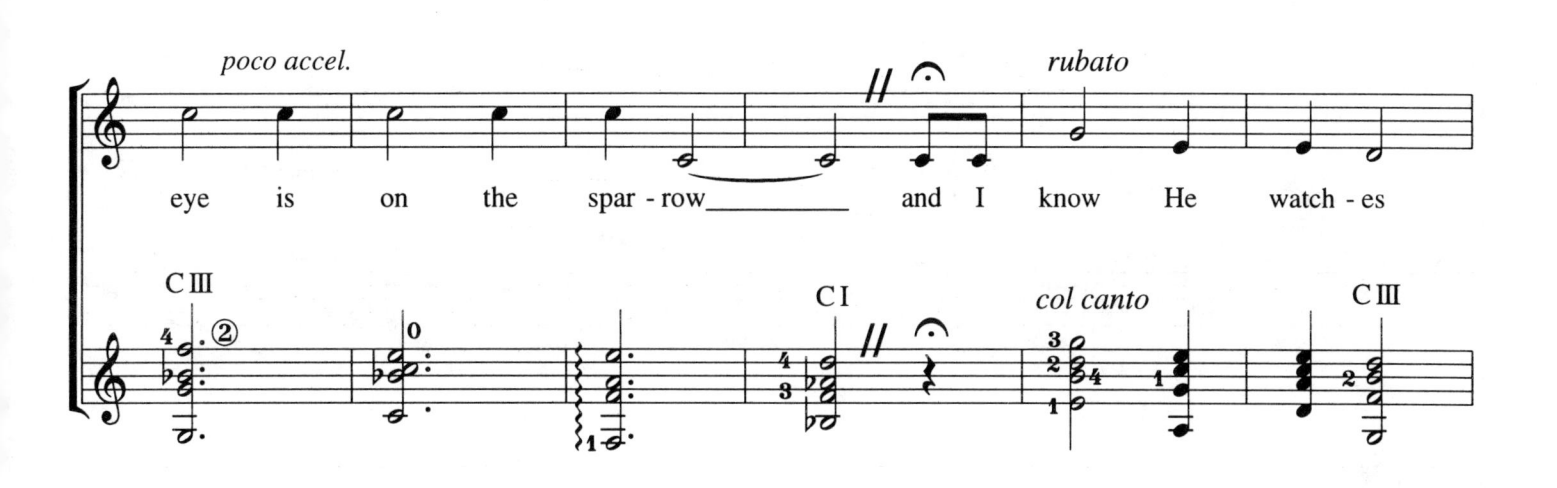

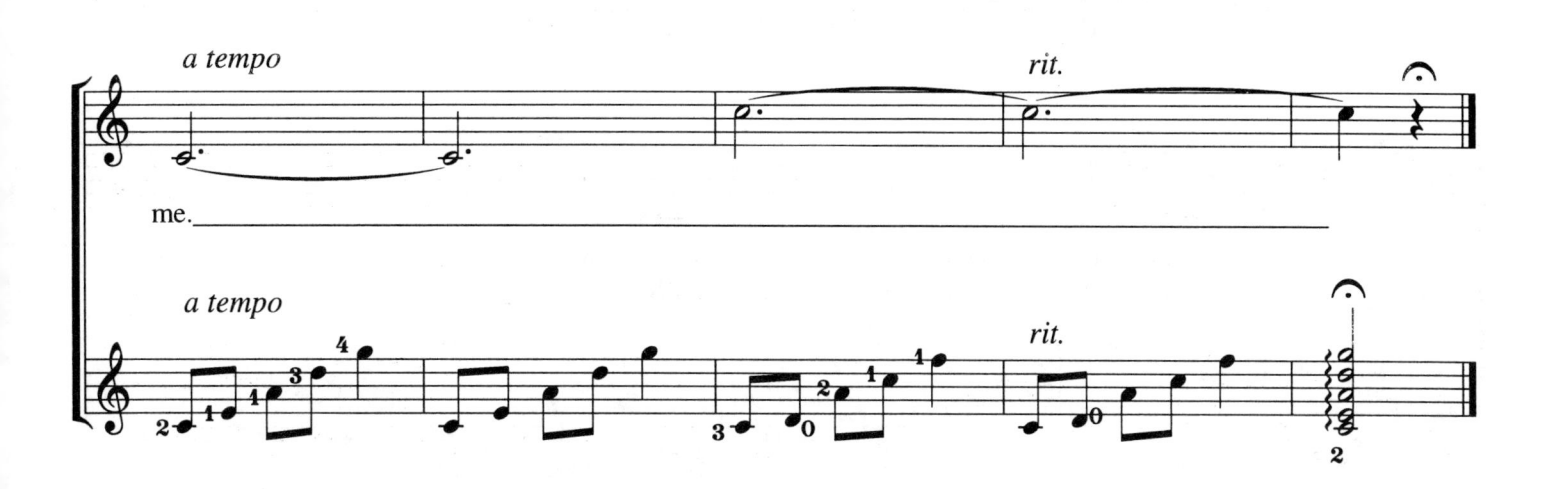

I sing be-cause I'm free. For His eye is on the spar-row and I know He watch-es me.

A Prayer
(En Prière)

Arranged for Voice and Guitar by
Laurindo Almeida

Gabriel Fauré
(1845-1924)

Moderato

Si la voix d'un en-fant peut mon-ter jus-qu'a
If the voice of a child can reach out to

Vous, ô mon Pè - re, E - cou-tez de Jé-
You, oh my Fa - ther, List-en to the

-sus, de-vant Vous à ge-noux, La pri - è - re!
prayer of Je-sus on His knees be - fore You!

Si Vous m'a-vez choi - si pour en-seig-ner Vos lois Sur la
If you have cho - sen me to teach Your laws on the

Copyright © 1996 Brazilliance Music. All Rights Reserved. Used by Permission. Exclusive Selling Agent: Mel Bay Publications, Inc.

ter - re, Je saurai Vous ser - vir. au - gus - te Roi des
earth I will Know how to serve You, ho - ly King of

Rois, Ô Lu - miè - re! Sur mes lè - vres, Sei -
Kings, O Light! On my lips

gneur, met - tez la vé - ri - té Sa - lu - tai - re
place the sal - u - ta - ry truth O Fath - er

Pour que ce - lui qui doute, a - vec hu - mi - li - té Vous ré -
So that who - ev - er doubts should with hu - mi - li - ty Re -

vè - re! Ne m'à-ban-don-nez pas, don-nez-moi la dou-
vere You! Do not a-ban-don me, give me gen - tle-

ceur Né - ces - sai - re, pour a - pai - ser les
ness ne - ces - sa - ry to re-lieve suf - fer-

maux, son-la-ger la dou-leur, La mi - se -
ing, to al - le - vi - ate pain, and mi - ser -

re! Ré - vè - lez Vous a moi, Sei - gneur en qui je
y! Re - veal Your-self to me O Lord in whom I

Poem of Stéphan Bordèse
English translation by Edith Braun and Waldo Hyman
(with a few subtle changes by Deltra Eamon, to make it easier to sing)

If the voice of a child can reach you,
O my Father,
Listen to the prayer of Jesus on His knees
Before You.
If You have chosen me to teach Your laws
On the earth,
I will know how to serve You, holy King of Kings,
O Light!
Place on my lips, O Lord,
The salutary truth,

So that whoever doubts, should with humility
Revere You!
Do not abandon me, give me the gentleness
So necessary
To relieve the suffering, to alleviate pains,
The misery!
Reveal Yourself to me, Lord, in whom I have faith
And hope,
I want to suffer for You and to die on the Cross,
At Calvary!

Amazing Grace

Traditional Early American Song
Arranged for Voice and Guitar by
Laurindo Almeida

1. A-maz-ing Grace how sweet the sound, That saved a wretch like me! I once was lost, but now am found, Was blind, but now I see.
2. grace that taught my heart to fear, And grace my fears re-lieved; How precious did that grace ap-pear The hour I first be-

Copyright © 1996 Brazilliance Music. All Rights Reserved. Used by Permission. Exclusive Selling Agent: Mel Bay Publications, Inc.

2. 'Twas lieved! 3. Through many dangers, toils and snares, I have already come; 'Tis grace has brought me safe thus far, And grace will lead me home.

4. The Lord has promised good to me, His word my hope secures; He will my shield and portion be As long as life endures.

Didi (Deltra Eamon) and Laurindo Almeida

Jesu, Joy of Man's Desiring
(from Cantata No. 147)

Arranged for Voice and Guitar by
Laurindo Almeida

J. S. Bach

Je - su, joy of man's de - sir - ing, ho - ly wis - dom love most bright drawn by Thee our souls as - pir - ing, soar to un - cre - a - ted light. Word of God our flesh that fa - shioned with the fire of life im - pas - sioned.

C *mf*
striv - - ing still to truth un - - - known.

p
soar - ing, dy - - ing round Thy throne.

D 11

Jesu, Joy of Man's Desiring
(from Cantata No. 147)

JOHANN SEBASTIAN BACH
Arranged for Solo Guitar by
Laurindo Almeida

Andante ♩ = 80

Jesu, joy of man's desiring,
Holy wisdom, love most bright
Drawn by Thee, our souls aspiring,
Soar to uncreated light.

Word of God our flesh that fashioned
With the fire of life impassioned,
Striving still to truth unknown,
Soaring, dying, round Thy throne.

Were You There When They Crucified My Lord?

(A Traditional Negro Spiritual)

Arranged for Voice and Guitar by
Laurindo Almeida

Quasi senza tempo

Lyrics:
1 there when they cru-ci-fied my Lord?
Were you 2 there when they nailed Him to the tree?
3 there when they laid Him in the tomb?

Were you there when they cru-ci-fied my Lord?
Were you there when they nailed Him to the tree? Oh!____
Were you there when they laid Him in the tomb?

Copyright © 1996 Brazilliance Music. All Rights Reserved. Used by Permission. Exclusive Selling Agent: Mel Bay Publications, Inc.

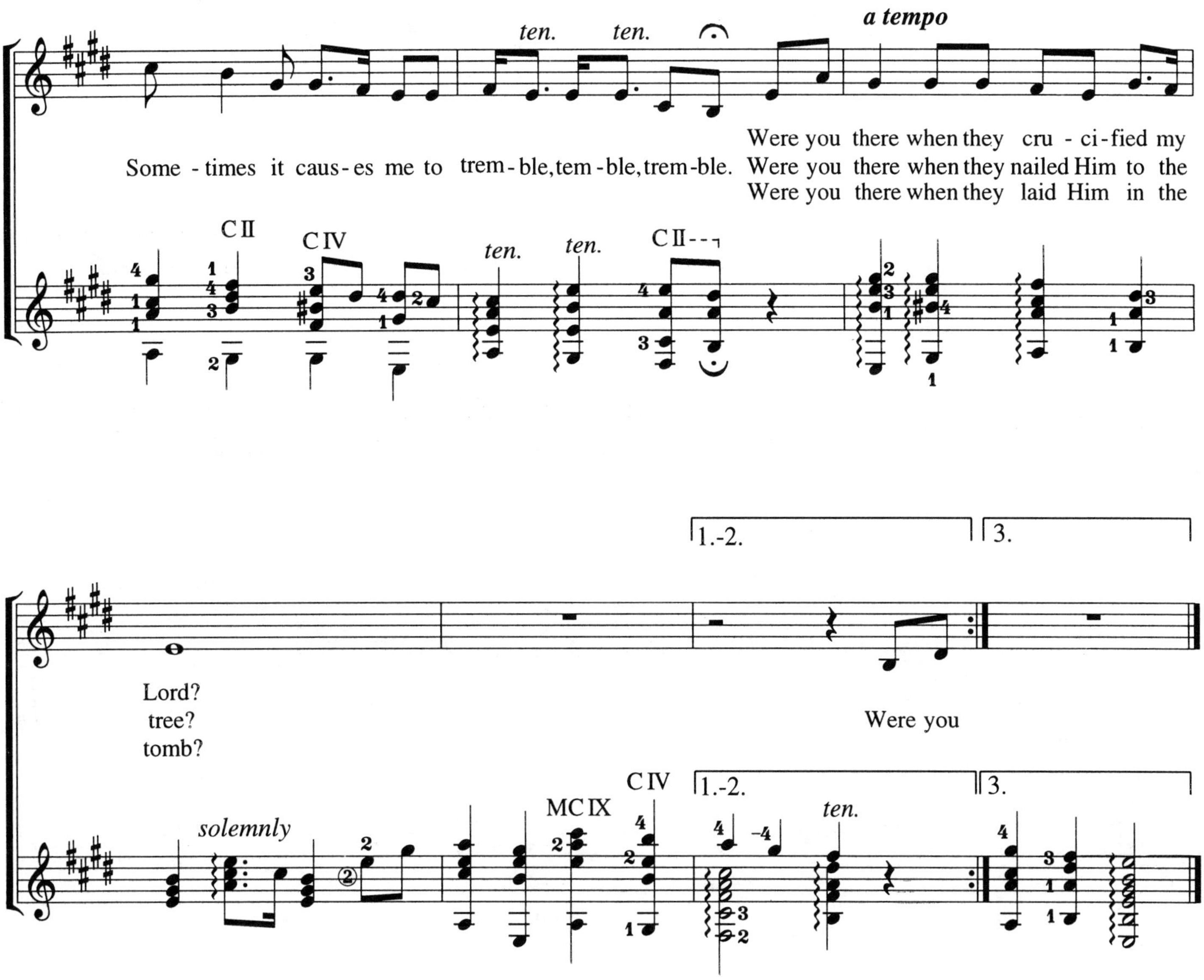
ten. ten.
a tempo
Were you there when they cru - ci-fied my
Some - times it caus-es me to trem-ble, tem-ble, trem-ble. Were you there when they nailed Him to the
Were you there when they laid Him in the
C II
C IV
ten. ten.
C II
1.-2.
3.
Lord?
tree?
tomb?
Were you
C IV
MC IX
solemnly
ten.

Jesus, Jesus, Rest Your Head
(A Christmas Song from the Appalachian Mountains)

Arranged for Voice and Guitar by
Laurindo Almeida

Copyright © 1996 Brazilliance Music. All Rights Reserved. Used by Permission. Exclusive Selling Agent: Mel Bay Publications, Inc.

Lyrics:

How His mam-my went to that sta-ble on that Christ-mas eve so late. Winds were blow-ing, cows were low-ing, stars were glow-ing, glow-ing, glow-ing. Je-sus, Je-sus, rest your head, you has got a man-ger bed.

To that sta-ble came three wise men

bearing gifts from hin and yon for the mother and the father and the blessed little son. Shepherds left their fields and flocks to sit beside the ass and ox. Jesus, Jesus, rest your head, you has got a manger bed. All the evil folk on earth sleep in feathers at their birth. Jesus, Jesus, rest your head, you has got a manger bed. Jesus, Jesus. Jesus, Jesus, rest your head, you has got a manger bed.

molto rit.

Nobody Knows The Trouble I've Seen

Arranged for Voice and Guitar by
Laurindo Almeida

Traditional Spiritual

times I'm up, Some - times I'm down, Oh! yes, Lord. Some -
C III
times I'm al - most to the ground Oh! yes, Lord. No-bod - y knows the
C III
trou-ble I've seen, No-bod - y knows but Je - sus, No-bod - y knows the
C III
trou-ble I've seen Glo - ry Hal - e - lu - jah! I
C II
C III

nev - er shall for - get that day Oh! yes, Lord. When Je - sus washed my
C VIII VI C II
sins a - way Oh! yes, Lord. No-bod - y knows the
C I C IV C VI C VI C IV
trou-ble I've seen, No-bod-y knows but Je - sus. No-bod-y knows the
C I C I C IV
poco rit.
trou-ble I've seen Glo - ry Hal - e - lu - jah!
C III C I C VI C II IV

What God Hath Promised

Music by
DELTRA and LAURINDO ALMEIDA
(A.S.C.A.P.)

Moderately and fervently

God hath not pro - mised skies al - ways blue
But God hath pro - mised strength for the day

flow - er strewn path - ways all our
rest from our la - bor and

Copyright © 1996 Brazilliance Music. All Rights Reserved. Used by Permission. Exclusive Selling Agent: Mel Bay Publications, Inc.

lives_____ through God hath not
light for our way Grace hath for our

pro - mised sun with - out___ rain.
tri - als help from a - bove.

1.
Joy with - out sor - row peace with - out_____ pain.

2.
un - fail - ing sym - pa - thy un - dy - ing

love Yes, Goth hath pro - mised

help from a - bove un - fail - ing

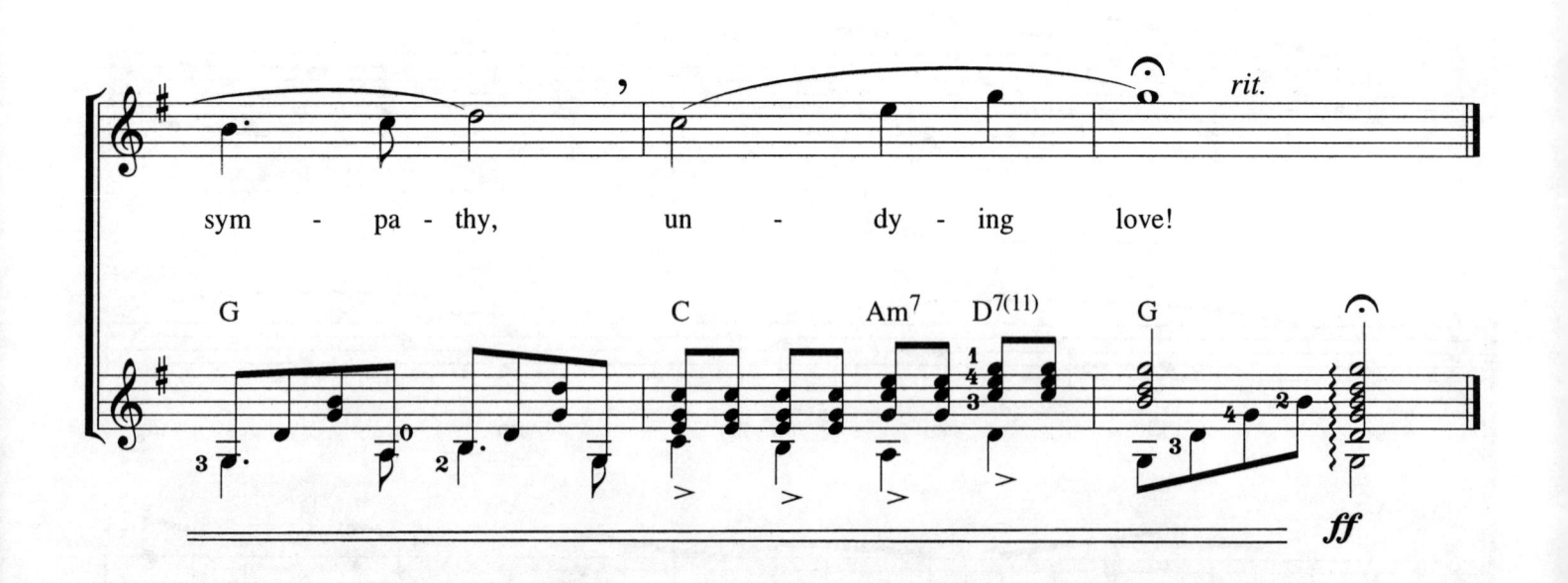

sym - pa - thy, un - dy - ing love!

Laurindo Almeida

MEL BAY

Great Music at Your Fingertips